49 Aphorisms
& a poem

K.C. Bacon

Copyright 2019 K.C. Bacon

All rights reserved. No part of this book may be reproduced in any form by any means electronic or mechanical, including photocopying, recording or by any information storage and retrieval systems, without written permission of the publisher or author except where permitted by law.

Bellus Books
Tacoma, Washington

First Edition

ISBN: 978-0-359-52864-6

Published in the USA

49 Aphorisms & a poem

Once again, for Lily

Elegance is ego
without arrogance.

Politics is a nasty virus produced by democracy, voters its antibiotic.

Hell is being ashamed
of not being in heaven.

Mockery is how a snob
delivers a cheap shot.

Doubt is the crap you step in
while entranced by yourself.

Second-guessing
is a journalistic fetish.

MENSA ought to be smarter than to exist.

Every emcee should dream
of being mayor.

Politics is how adults retain their adolescent dignity.

When you get on the wrong side of yourself,
you lose twice.

When your libido finally runs off with your ego, change your locks.

Jazz and baseball are twins
from the best family in town.

A celebrity is humanity's punchline.

When you get on the wrong side of yourself,
you lose twice.

When your libido finally runs off with your ego, change your locks.

The self
is a wary comrade.

Talking to yourself can be entertaining, unless your talking with someone else.

If the NRA were into gun safety,
why does it so often shoot itself in the foot?

A weak sentence is a stream
where invasive adjectives spawn.

The nightly news is news
with a bad facelift.

False modesty is
the show-off's quiet twin.

Narcissism is a
zero sum game.

More people fall off high horses
than ride them.

Discourtesy is
a good deed lost.

Nothing is more complex
than the obvious.

Good intentions are essential for bad poetry.

Nothing excites a politician's nose more than the sniff of ignorance.

The best beach bums
don't actually need a beach.

Contempt of others is how one displays contempt for oneself.

If an artist can't draw,
the duel won't go well.

A dagger is best hid
by a compliment.

For the moralist and the loudmouth, being disagreeable is an exercise in truth-formation.

To have an independent mind
you must first not leave a mess.

What we imagine is sometimes the result of having a bad imagination.

No saint is a saint
during adolescence.

The biggest problem with emotions
is they get too emotional.

Hatred loves nothing,
and nothing loves it back.

Good neighbors are worth the effort,
even if it requires a bribe.

Common sense is never hip,
its too sensible for that.

Problems echo
their solutions.

Even bad days
have their good days.

People who shout
are nothing to shout about.

Every man wishes to be King, but they can't because there can only be one King, and its me.

Cleverness is often malice pretending to be kind.

Lots of characters
have no character.

Agile powers of recovery
makes sobriety easier to suffer.

To disregard God
is to misread consciousness.

Truths are never found,
just uncovered.

Emotion is the rabbit,
Reason its turtle.

Humility is the role
than won the ego its Oscar.

Every former miser has been successful at least once.

A POEM

Why strive for worth and meter,
So that we may arrive at the Pearly Gate
And get ushered in by St. Peter.

Better to be wholly human, sad and funny
Battling the devil
While enjoying his money.

About the Author

K.C. Bacon was born in Aiea Ewa, Hawaii in 1948, and raised in a Navy family in England, Rhode Island, Virginia, California, and Corvallis, Oregon. Graduating from Oregon State University and attending Pacific School of Religion in Berkeley, California, he subsequently spent 35 years in the Pacific Northwest stevedoring industry. His artwork can be seen at www.kcbacon.com.